It's Normal to be Different

Rolling Through Life With Muscular Dystrophy

Erika Daisy Wrate

First published 2025 by Wrate's Publishing

ISBN 978-1-917970-02-0

Copyright © Erika Daisy Wrate

Edited and typeset by Wrate's Editing Services
www.wrateseditingservices.co.uk

The right of Erika Daisy Wrate to be identified as the author of this work has been asserted in accordance with the Copyright, Designs and Patents Act, 1988.

All rights reserved. No part of this publication may be reproduced, stored in a retrieval system, or transmitted, in any form or by any means (electronic, mechanical, photocopying, recording or otherwise), without the prior written permission of the publisher.

A CIP catalogue record for this book is available from the British Library.

Contents

Introduction   5
  My Diagnosis   7
  The Wheelchairs Arrive!   9
  Starting School   11
  Finding the Right Support: My Carers   13
  Sharks and Fishes   15
  Secondary School and GCSEs   17
  The Perks of Homeschooling   20
  Family and Home Adjustments   22
  Operations and Hospital Stays   24
  Managing My Epilepsy   27
  New Equipment and Evolving Care   29
  My Day-to-Day Routine   32
  Friendships Through the Years   34
  The Annual Visit from Santa   41
  Trips to Jersey   43
  London Visits and Family Time   46
  Trips to Lincoln and Sleepovers at Sam's   47
  Sundown Adventureland and the Yellow Brick Road   49
  Family Holidays – Well Worth the Wait   50
  Burghley House: Gardens, Mazes and Family Memories   52
  Seals, Sand and Unforgettable Adventures   53
  Discovering Musicals and the West End   56

BBC Good Food Festival	59
Welcoming Toby, the Chocolate Labrador	61
Homemade Comfort: Meals with My Grandparents	63
Crafting Memories: Jewellery, Baking and Getting Creative	65
My Creative Journey: Handmade By EDW	67
Special Birthday Memories	69
Lockdown Fun	71
Another Member Joins the Family	73
Keeping Traditions Alive	81
Humpty: The Unexpected Mascot	84
Fun Times with Eva	85
Adventures at The Parrot Zoo	86
Center Parcs Trips and Traditions	88
A Cosy Cotswolds Getaway	90
Living Room Concerts and Off-Key Duets	92
Barney the Dinosaur	94
ABBA-solutely Living My Best Life	96
Epilogue	100

Introduction

Ever since I was little, my family has commented that my views on life and being in a wheelchair are unique. For me, my chair is just a piece of equipment, and my disability – congenital muscular dystrophy – is just a part of who I am. Neither has ever stopped me from going places with my friends and family or chasing after my dreams, whether that's starting my own business or writing this book.

I've always had my own way of looking at the world, and there have been plenty of times when I've completely lost my parents in conversation. I'll start talking about something that makes perfect sense in my head, but halfway through, Mum or Dad will stop me and ask, "What are you actually talking about?" By that point, I'll just say, "Forget it," because, honestly, even I don't know anymore.

One Christmas, my late grandma bought me a magnet that says, "It's an Erika thing, you wouldn't understand," and to this day, it's the most accurate description of me. There are so many moments when I say or do things that make sense only to me, and everyone else is left trying to figure out what's going on.

Take weekend dinners, for instance – if the conversation gets a bit boring for me, I tend to switch off, stare into space, and drift into my own little world. After a few minutes, Mum, Dad, or my brother Sam will gently nudge me back and ask what I was thinking about. Most of the time, I tell them I was mentally replaying songs I'd been listening to. It's like I have a built-in radio that randomly shuffles through my favourite tunes. And sometimes, after reassuring everyone I'm fine, I'll go straight back to my musical daydream like nothing happened!

It's just the way my brain works – a little bit chaotic, often entertaining, and definitely one of a kind. My memoir is a collection of stories which, rather like my internal playlist, I often find myself returning to when I've drifted off around the dinner table. Now I've decided to share them and show that, whether you've been touched by disability or not, it's normal to be different.

My Diagnosis

Congenital Muscular Dystrophy (CMD) – or, as I used to call it when I was younger, *Muscular Difficulties* – is a muscle weakness condition that affects me in many ways and has shaped who I am. I was diagnosed at just six months old, but even before that, Mum had already started to notice that something wasn't quite right.

When I was at nursery, all the other babies would be rolling around, waving their arms, and causing mayhem, but I was always just lying on my back, happily giggling at the chaos around me. Mum also noticed that I couldn't sit up without support, and while she had a feeling that something was different, she wasn't sure what it was. She and Dad decided to take me to the doctor for a check-up, hoping for some answers.

To officially diagnose me, the doctors performed a muscle biopsy. The results confirmed that I had CMD. It was a huge shock for my parents, as they had never even heard of the condition before. Suddenly, they were thrown into a world of medical terminology, hospital visits, and uncertainty about what the future would look like for me.

At the time, Mum was working as a primary school teacher, a job she loved. But after my diagnosis, she made the incredibly difficult decision to leave her career so she could take care of me full-time. She dedicated her spare time to researching, talking to doctors, and learning everything she could about my condition.

Growing up with CMD has meant adapting to things differently, but it has never stopped me from living life to the fullest. From a young age, I had to learn how to navigate the world in my own way, finding ways to do things that worked for me. My family has always been my biggest support system, making sure I never felt limited by my condition.

Although my muscles may not work the way other people's do, I've never let that define me. Over the years, I've found so much joy in the things I love, whether that's baking, crafting, music, or spending time with my family and friends. I've also learned that having a disability doesn't mean missing out on things; it just means finding creative ways to make them happen.

Looking back now, I realise how much my journey with CMD has shaped me – not just in terms of the challenges I've faced, but also in the strength, resilience, and incredible experiences it has brought into my life. And if there's one thing I've learned, it's that sometimes the biggest obstacles can lead to the most unexpected and beautiful adventures.

The Wheelchairs Arrive!

And then came the wheelchairs – first, a manual one, and then an electric one. My first electric wheelchair came from a company called Whizz Kidz, and I think the name perfectly describes what I was like when I was younger: always zooming around and full of energy.

My electric wheelchair gave me a whole new sense of independence. I could finally move around on my own without needing someone to push me. Sure, there were a few minor collisions along the way – mostly with people's toes (oops). Honestly, I think my wheelchair has a secret hatred for feet, because somehow, I always managed to find them. If my wheelchair could talk, it would probably say, "Target locked! Impact in 3... 2... 1. Sorry, not sorry." Let's just say, I didn't need to take a driving test to figure out that running over people's tootsies wasn't ideal.

To be fair, at that age, I didn't even know what a driving test was or what it meant! But hey, at least my wheelchair didn't come with speeding tickets.

Along with people's toes, my poor house took quite a beating. Door frames were bashed into, cupboard doors pulled off. When I used my sling and hoist, the straps seemed to have a mind of their own. A sling is a piece of fabric that supports me while I'm being lifted with a hoist – but apparently, mine doubled as a demolition tool. More than once, I'd be whizzing around when my sling strap latched onto a cupboard handle, and before I knew it, I'd be dragging the cupboard door along with me!

Dad became quite the expert in home repairs, whether he wanted to or not.

Starting School

When it was time for me to start primary school, it wasn't as simple as Mum dropping me off at the gates and me rolling into class like everyone else. There was a lot to sort out first. While other kids were busy choosing their backpacks, my parents were busy working with the school to figure out how I could actually attend.

Could my wheelchair fit through the doors? Were there ramps? Could they make space for my equipment? And how would I get around during the day? These were all questions that had to be answered before I could even step – well, roll – into my first classroom.

I couldn't go to the same primary school as my brother, Sam, who is three years older than me, because it wasn't wheelchair-friendly. Instead, I went to a school that was more accessible. They even custom built a bathroom, complete with a hoist and a plinth, just to make things easier for me.

Another big thing was that I needed a carer at school to help me with day-to-day things like getting around, using my equipment, and making sure I was included in everything. It was a lot to organise, but eventually, everything was in place, and I could properly start school.

One of the best parts of primary school was when Dad, who was a school photographer then, came in to take our class photos. If he finished before lunch, he'd pack up his equipment and come and have lunch with me. Getting to sit with Dad in the middle of the school day while everyone else just had their usual routine was a nice little treat.

Finding the Right Support: My Carers

While attending primary and secondary school, I was provided with carers to help me through my day. In primary school, my carer was a lovely lady called Mrs Smith. Even now, she still sends me cards on my birthday and at Christmas.

When I moved on to secondary school, things became trickier. The school selected the carers on my behalf, but they weren't always the best people for the job, as their knowledge of my disability and how to care for me was limited. That's when Mum decided to take matters into her own hands. We started choosing and interviewing people for the role ourselves, asking them what they knew about muscular dystrophy and whether they'd had any experience looking after kids like me. This completely turned the situation around and made my last two years at school less stressful, as I had the support I needed.

When I left school to be homeschooled, the carer we had chosen for my final years at school, Linda, continued her role, this time looking after me at home. It was great to have that consistency, as I was already comfortable with her, and she really understood my needs.

When Linda left, we had to find someone to take over. That's when Mum saw on Facebook that her cousin Jane was looking for a similar role, so we offered her the job, and she accepted! She's a great person to have take care of me, and sometimes I get to hear stories about her and Mum when they were my age, which always makes me laugh.

Over the years, I've had a couple of different carers, but each one I've had has been the best for the job. When I was 14, Mum also decided I needed an overnight carer because she was struggling to take care of me both during the day and at night. This carer, Sharon, had already used all my medical equipment in her previous jobs, which made the transition much easier.

Sharks and Fishes

When I was younger, me, Sam and Mum would go to our local pool – and one of my favourite games was *Sharks and Fishes*. During this game, Mum would float me around the pool while Sam would go underwater and try to grab my feet. It was always so much fun, and I'd try my best to avoid him – even though he was pretty fast!

As the years went by and I learned to swim – or in my case, float – I also mastered how to go underwater. I used to really enjoy doing this because it felt so peaceful. The pool would sometimes get busy, with people splashing and chatting, but once under the water, everything went quiet. It was a nice break from the noise – even though I didn't stay for long. I'd always do a little wiggle when I was ready to come back up, so Mum knew I needed air.

After our swim, Mum would take Sam and me across the road to a small café, where we'd have our favourite meal – fish fingers, smiley face chips and baked beans. If we were good, we'd get a special treat of raspberry sorbet for dessert. It was the perfect end to a fun swim, and I looked forward to it every time.

I often think that Mum took us swimming to tire us out for the afternoon or evening. Whether it was to wear us out before bedtime – or just to give us something active to do – it seemed like the perfect way to keep us busy and happy.

Swimming wasn't just fun for me, though – it was also really relaxing. Being in the water allowed my whole body to stretch out and float, which made me feel light and calm. The water always made me feel weightless – like I was floating freely. The combination of fun, relaxation and time spent with family made swimming one of my all-time favourite activities.

Secondary School and GCSEs

Secondary school wasn't the right fit for me, and I was keen to leave as soon as possible. Mum told me that once I passed my GCSEs, I'd be homeschooled, which was a big relief. My first attempt at taking my GCSEs didn't go well, but Mum got me a tutor she knew from her teaching days. With her help, I was able to pass the second time around and start the next phase of my life.

I guess being at secondary school wasn't all bad. In my final year, I enjoyed lunchtime because I could go to the local shops and buy a Subway. There were also some lessons I found fun, like food technology. Mum liked that one too, as it meant she didn't have to cook tea on those days! I also enjoyed art, although it did irritate me at times. Because of my disability, the school decided I wasn't able to do some tasks independently, such as using art equipment or materials like sketching pencils or clay, which I found frustrating. It didn't stop me from trying, but it did make me feel underestimated.

My Prom: Not Quite the Fairytale

Like most teenagers, I had a vision of what my secondary school prom was going to be like. I imagined a magical evening that involved getting dressed up, having fun with my friends, dancing to great music, and making unforgettable memories. In my head, it was going to be like something out of a movie, where everyone was having the time of their lives, and the night felt truly special.

But reality didn't quite match up to that vision.

For starters, the build-up to prom wasn't particularly exciting for me. While most of my classmates were busy planning their outfits, talking about getting their hair and makeup done, and discussing who they were going with, I didn't feel as involved in all of that. Since I didn't have the best experience at secondary school, I wasn't surrounded by a big group of friends, so there wasn't that same level of excitement for me. To add to my disappointment, my best friend Morgan had changed schools by this point because she hadn't got on there either. Without her, the idea of prom wasn't so appealing.

Then came the actual night. I arrived, expecting to feel a buzz in the air, but instead, it felt underwhelming. The atmosphere wasn't as electric as I'd hoped, and a lot of people stuck to their usual friendship groups. I had imagined a night where everyone came together to celebrate the end of an era, but instead, it just felt like any other school event, except everyone was in fancy clothes.

The music wasn't great either, which didn't help. I had pictured a playlist full of fun, upbeat songs that would have everyone on the dancefloor, but the tunes were a letdown, and there wasn't as much dancing as I'd imagined.

I did my best to enjoy the night, but it was soon clear that it wasn't going to be the magical, movie-style experience I had imagined. Looking back, I don't regret going, but I also don't see it as one of the highlights of my teenage years. If anything, it taught me an important lesson: sometimes, the things we build up in our heads don't always turn out the way we expect, and that's OK.

At the end of the day, my prom wasn't about the event itself, but a reminder that school was finally over, and I was moving on to bigger and better things.

The Perks of Homeschooling

Homeschooling turned out to be a much more enjoyable experience compared to the traditional school system. The flexibility it offered was a huge advantage, and I quickly adapted to the new routine. My lessons were scheduled for the end of the school day, and the work was manageable, allowing me to go at my own pace. Without the pressure of a typical school environment, I found myself learning in a way that suited me. My tutor, Lindsay, was not only amazing at her job but also became a great friend. I even became friends with her daughter, Orla. It was also funny to learn that Lindsay had been a primary school teacher at the same time as my mum – she even taught Sam at one point, which we often laughed about.

Another big perk of homeschooling was the extra time it gave me to develop and explore my hobbies. I could dive into activities like reading, writing, and drawing. These pastimes became an important part of my daily routine and allowed me to express myself in ways I'd never had the chance to do before. Whether it was getting lost in a book, jotting down my thoughts, or creating something on paper, my creative outlets provided a sense of fulfilment that the classroom couldn't offer. I felt more connected to myself and my interests, and it gave me a sense of pride and joy to pursue them without any external pressure.

The absolute highlight of homeschooling was the meals. Unlike the cafeteria food at school, I could now enjoy homemade dinners. On Fridays, we even treated ourselves to a pub lunch. This small but meaningful change felt like a real treat. It was nice to have the flexibility to enjoy good food and quality time with loved ones instead of rushing through a school lunch break. Plus, being able to eat out regularly felt like a huge upgrade from the usual school routine.

Beyond the academic side, homeschooling offered me the space and time to grow as an individual. It was a chance to focus on my wellbeing, explore my passions, and find a balance that worked for me.

Family and Home Adjustments

As I got older and heavier, our home had to be adapted. A downstairs bedroom was built to accommodate all my equipment and essentials, including an electric bed and a ceiling-mounted hoist to help lift me up and down. When I'm in my sling on the hoist, it feels a bit like being on a giant swing. My new room also has patio doors that open out into the garden, which is lovely all year round – bright and open in summer, peaceful and cosy in winter. At the same time, we also built an extension for my grandad and grandma so they could have their own space while still being close to us.

As well as making adjustments for my needs – and my grandparents' – we also built something purely for fun (and our peace and quiet!). When my dad was in his mid-twenties, he was a DJ in pubs and clubs, and his love of music has definitely rubbed off on me – something I'm grateful for. But with that passion came the habit of playing music *very* loudly for long stretches of time. When I was little and Mum was trying to get me to sleep, all we could hear was the steady *duff, duff, duff* of the bass. So, that's when we came up with a plan: we turned one of the sheds into a pub. That way, Dad could crank the volume as high as he liked without it bothering us – and we could host parties in there too! And if anyone needed a break, or I'd had enough of the noise, we could retreat to the nice, quiet house.

Over the years, we've added to the pub to make it even better. One of the first things we installed was a pizza oven, thanks to my brother getting really into pizza-making. He was always in the kitchen, experimenting with different doughs and toppings.

Later, we added a patio area at the back that overlooks the fields – a perfect spot to relax in the summer and enjoy the view. It makes the pub feel like an ideal gathering place for family and friends.

We also built a cinema room in the garden. Our local cinema wasn't wheelchair-friendly, so creating our own felt like the perfect solution. It became a cosy space where we could enjoy movie nights together without having to worry about access.

Another change we made was to the lounge. We decided to divide it and turn part of it into a home office for me. That way, I wasn't spending the whole day in my bedroom, and I had a dedicated space to focus when I needed to work. It made a big difference – giving me a change of scenery and helping to separate work from relaxation.

Operations and Hospital Stays

Alongside growing up, my health needs changed, and I began spending many winters in hospital, mostly due to chest infections. It wasn't fun, but when you have muscular dystrophy and come down with something, hospital really is the best place to be.

I also had to stay overnight for sleep studies to monitor my breathing levels. The test itself was straightforward – I had to wear a small clip on either my finger or toe, which was connected to a machine that tracked my breathing rate and oxygen levels while I slept. Getting a full night's rest in a hospital bed wasn't easy, especially with all the noise and interruptions, and being away from home made it harder to relax. But as I got older, things got a little easier – particularly when my brother Sam started working for my dad.

At that time, I was still on the paediatric ward at Nottingham Hospital, which was close to Dad's factory. So, when Sam finished work, he could pop by the hospital, pick up the sleep study machine, and bring it home for the weekend. That meant I could do the test from the comfort of my own bed, and Sam would return the equipment to the hospital on his way back to the factory. It worked perfectly and made the whole process far less stressful for everyone.

As I transitioned from paediatric to adult care, organising sleep studies became much more difficult. The paediatric nurses used to meet us halfway between QMC in Nottingham and our home near Skegness to hand over the Tosca machine, but the adult team doesn't offer this. It's a long journey for Mum and me to collect and return the equipment, but we're finding ways around it – and when all's said and done, it's still better than having to stay overnight in hospital.

One of the biggest things Mum, Dad and the doctors noticed around the time I turned ten was how thin I was getting. As I grew, I wasn't gaining weight because I couldn't eat enough. That's when the decision was made to fit a gastrostomy peg – a feeding device attached to my stomach – to help me get the nutrients I needed.

Another major concern was that my spine was beginning to twist. Not only was this uncomfortable, but it was also making my chest infections worse, as one lung was being squashed by the curvature. The medical name for a twisted spine is *scoliosis*, and to correct it, I needed surgery to straighten my spine using a metal rod. There was a catch, though – I had to gain a certain amount of weight first to make the operation safer. That's where the feeding peg became essential. It helped me put on the weight I needed just in time for the scoliosis surgery, which I had when I was eleven.

The surgery was a major one. Towards the end, I started to lose too much blood, so the doctors had to stop before they could fully straighten the lower part of my spine. This meant I would still have a slight curve, but overall, the operation made a huge difference to my health and comfort.

To help with breathing during surgery and recovery, I had a tracheostomy fitted – a small tube placed in my throat to help me breathe. But it affected my vocal cords and, for a short time, I wasn't able to speak. I had to come up with my own kind of sign language, mostly pointing to a word board the nurses gave me. It sounds simple, but it really wasn't. If I was in pain or needed something, I had to try to tell Mum using the board, which was frustrating and exhausting for both of us. It wasn't easy, but Mum stayed calm and patient, and together we found ways to get through it.

During the scoliosis operation, some of the nerves near my hips were affected, and ever since, I've had a weird, persistent numbness in that area – sometimes with a pins-and-needles feeling. It's something I've just had to learn to live with.

After the surgery, I had to re-learn how to feel comfortable sitting upright. The metal rod made me feel quite stiff at first, and that took some adjusting to. But over time, I adapted. The most important thing was that my spine was straighter, which made breathing much easier.

Sam's visits during my hospital stay were always something I looked forward to. One visit in particular still makes me laugh. That day, he'd been at the beach with his friends, soaking up the sun and sea. When he got to the hospital, he didn't hesitate to jump straight into bed with me for a cuddle. Sweet, right? Well... not when he brought half the beach with him. There was sand everywhere – in the bed, under the covers, even on me. That's brothers for you!

Managing My Epilepsy

When I was in primary school, I developed epilepsy, which caused me to have seizures and something I used to call 'doos'. At first, it was a scary and confusing time for both me and my family as we tried to understand what was happening and how best to manage it. Thankfully, with the help of kind and knowledgeable doctors and specialists, I was given medication that helped control the seizures, which was a huge relief.

As I got older and my body changed, my medication and dosage were adjusted to match my age, weight and overall health. These changes helped keep the treatment effective, and regular check-ups allowed the doctors to monitor my progress. Knowing that my medical team was always keeping an eye on things gave us all peace of mind.

Alongside the medication, the doctors gave us helpful advice on how to prevent and manage seizures. This included simple things like avoiding bright or flashing lights – especially in the evenings – and making sure I got enough rest. I came to realise that managing epilepsy wasn't just about taking medicine; it was also about making sensible changes to my daily routine to support my overall health.

Another important part of my healthcare has been my feeding peg. It's helped in more ways than I ever expected. Not only does it ensure I get the nutrients I need, but it also helps keep my blood sugar levels steady. Keeping these levels balanced has reduced the number of seizures I experience and made it easier to stay on top of my condition.

With all of these things working together – medication, lifestyle changes, good nutrition and regular check-ups – I've been able to manage my health more effectively and focus on the things I enjoy.

Recently, after having a seizure that lasted a few minutes (including the recovery time), the doctors decided to prescribe me a recovery pen. It's a new step in my treatment plan, but one that made sense, especially as some of my seizures can go on a little longer. The pen is used if a seizure lasts longer than five minutes. If that happens, my family or carers can press the pen against the inside of my gum, which will help to stop the seizure and bring me back to a stable state more quickly.

It's been a huge relief for both me and my family to have this extra tool. It gives me peace of mind as I go about my day, knowing there's an added layer of protection in case something unexpected happens. Having the recovery pen isn't something I ever thought I'd need, but now that I do, I can really see how valuable it is. It's just one more way my doctors are making sure I receive the best care possible.

New Equipment and Evolving Care

By the time I was 14, living with a gastrostomy peg had become completely normal –just another part of my daily routine. Around the same time, I was also given a ventilator, which turned out to be a real lifesaver – literally!

These new additions made a huge difference to my health. The feeding peg ensured I got the nutrients I needed, especially during the winter months, when staying well always felt a bit harder. It also made taking medication much easier, whether it was headache tablets, painkillers, or my epilepsy treatment. And best of all, I could still eat normally, which was brilliant because I love food! On days when I wasn't feeling great, it was reassuring to know that my body was still getting everything it needed.

The ventilator was a game changer, particularly at night. It helped me breathe more easily and gave my lungs the support they needed while I slept. Between the peg and the ventilator, those long winter hospital stays became far less frequent. If I did pick up a chest infection, my body now had the backup it needed to fight it off.

Having a metal rod attached to my spine has also brought big improvements to my health and comfort. I do still need to be mindful of how long I stay in my chair – just like anyone else, my back needs time to rest too. But overall, the benefits of the surgery far outweigh any of the day-to-day challenges, and we've all noticed a huge improvement in my wellbeing.

When I was younger, a physiotherapist used to visit regularly to check on me. She explained that because I wasn't walking, my ankles were beginning to twist, which could cause problems later on. To help prevent this, the doctors recommended splints – removable casts designed to keep my ankles in the right position and stop them from twisting any further.

Oddly enough, getting fitted for the splints was actually quite fun! The process started with making a plaster cast of my feet to get the perfect shape. It was a bit messy, but I found it fascinating to watch. Once the moulds were done, I got to choose a colour or design for the splints. That part was definitely the best bit – it made the whole thing feel more personal and less medical. Adding a touch of creativity to something so practical made wearing the splints feel a bit more bearable.

But over time, remembering to wear them became a bit of a hassle. It was a daily reminder of something else I had to manage, and it started to feel more like a chore. As I got older, we decided that since I wasn't walking, a slight twist in my ankles wasn't really a big deal. Rather than stressing about keeping everything 'just right', we shifted focus to what really mattered: living life without unnecessary pressure. The splints had served their purpose, but eventually, easing up on perfection made more sense – and that decision brought its own kind of relief.

Finding the Right fit

Because of the slight twist in my feet, finding comfortable shoes has always been a bit of a challenge. Unless it was absolutely necessary, I usually opted for wearing two pairs of socks instead. But during the winter, that wasn't ideal. Indoors, I could keep my feet warm by sitting by the fire or using a hot water bottle, but outside they'd freeze.

A couple of years ago, Mum was scrolling through Facebook when she came across a company called Billy Footwear. They make shoes with a zip that goes all the way around the top, so instead of having to force your foot in, you simply unzip the shoe completely, place your foot inside, and zip it back up. The company was co-founded by a man named Billy, who became paralysed from the chest down after an accident. Facing the same difficulty with shoes himself, he designed this adaptive style to make getting dressed much easier.

Something as simple as finding the right footwear has made a surprisingly big difference. Now I can wear trainers and boots without worrying about squashed toes or aching feet – and best of all, I don't have to put up with freezing toes in the winter!

My Day-to-Day Routine

Let me give you a glimpse into my daily routine. While it can vary depending on the time of year, my plans, and how I'm feeling – there are some constants.

On a workday, I typically wake up around 7:30 am. Either Mum or Sharon helps me get started by hooking me up to a machine that gives me a set amount of water to keep me hydrated. I also receive my Fresubin (liquid food) through my gastrostomy peg for breakfast. Once I've eaten, Mum or Sharon helps me get dressed for the day.

At 9 am, my daytime carer, Jane, takes over. I stay in bed until about 10 am, and then Jane hoists me into my chair, and I head over to my office to begin work – which usually involves painting for my business. Around 1 pm, I go to the kitchen to meet Mum and choose my lunch. Then I return to bed to rest my back and have another bottle of Fresubin along with my lunch (this might vary on weekends or holidays). At about 2:30 pm, Jane helps me get back into my chair and then leaves for the day.

Technology has become an incredibly helpful tool for me – giving me a real sense of independence. It allows me to read and write, play games like Scrabble, and even create digital artwork. It's also really useful when I'm in my bedroom on my own and need to contact Mum – for instance, if I've dropped my phone or iPad, I can just ask Siri to FaceTime her. Another funny thing is that because Sam and I grew up with iPads and iPhones, we've become the household tech support. If something isn't working properly and Mum or Dad can't figure it out – they know that either Sam or I will!

In the afternoons, I usually watch TV. During the colder months, we have the log fire on – which makes it even cosier. Tea time is around 5 pm, and after Mum and Dad have had their meal, Mum gives me my third and final bottle of Fresubin for the day. If I'm extra hungry, she might give me a little more around 8:45 pm. At 9, Sharon takes over from Mum, and by 10, I'm ready for bed.

My routine follows a similar pattern throughout the week – although Friday is typically my day off. As most people are working, Mum and I take full advantage of the quieter atmosphere to go out – either shopping, to the cinema, or out for a meal. On Saturdays and Sundays, we stay home and bake together. We also catch up with Sam when he's visiting. This routine shifts a bit when we're on holiday, but overall, that's a typical day in my life.

Friendships Through the Years

When I was in primary school, like many kids, I made lots of friends. Over time, many of those friendships naturally faded, but one friend from those early days has stayed in my life – Morgan. We're still close now, and I really value the fact that she's stuck around.

Another long-standing friendship is with Alice, who is also a family friend. My mum is friends with her mum, Gill; my dad knows her dad, Neil; and my brother is friends with her sister, Emily. Being close to both Alice and Morgan has given me some brilliant memories over the years. When we were younger, we had loads of fun sleepovers and trips out. They've always been there for me, and I truly appreciate that. Whenever I'm unwell or just not feeling myself, they'll check in with a message, and sometimes even pop round for a visit.

Now that we're older, we enjoy catching up at restaurants or pubs, and they often come over for a drink or pizza night. Even though we don't see each other as often in person, social media has made it easier to stay connected and keep our friendships strong.

I've also become good friends with my brother's girlfriend, Olivia. We often meet up in Lincoln for lunch, and sometimes she comes home with Sam at the weekend. We love baking together – it's always a fun way to spend time. It's really lovely having Olivia in my life, and our friendship has become something I genuinely treasure.

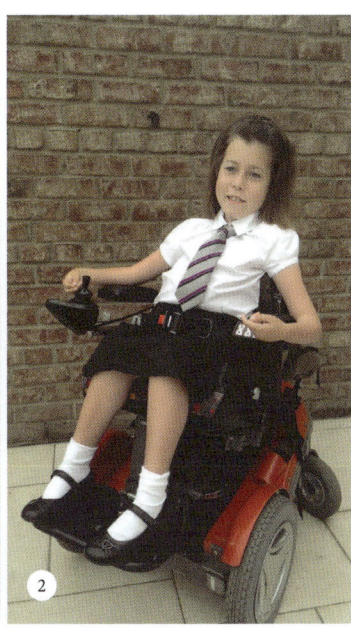

1. The early chapters 2. School days
3. The surgery experience

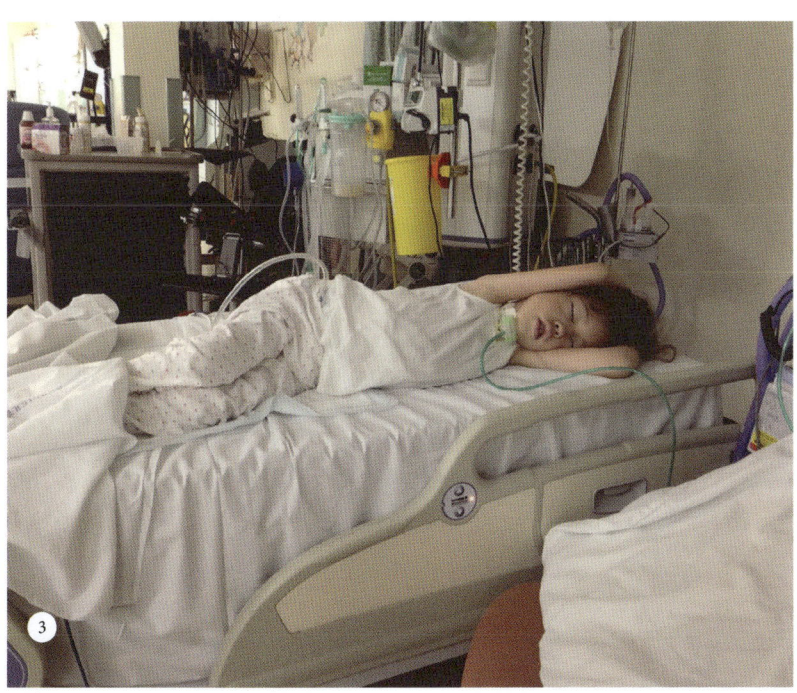

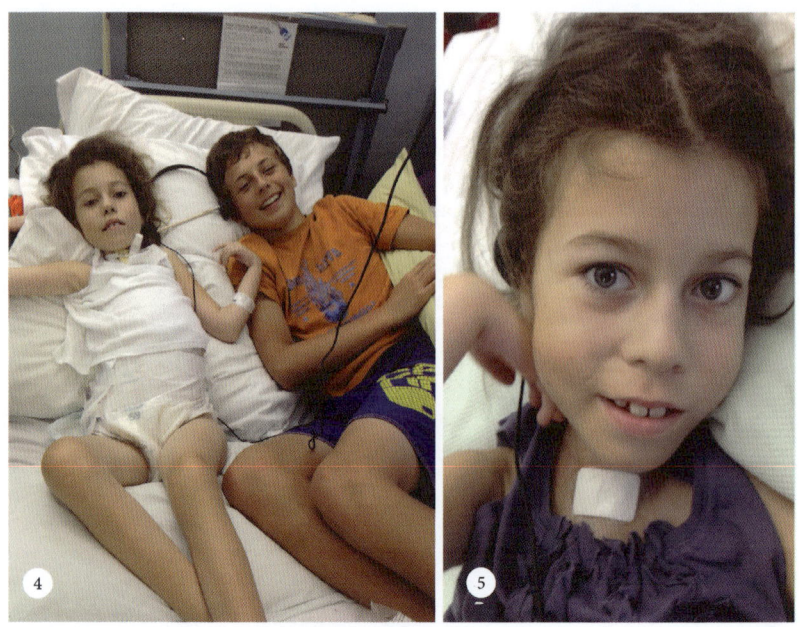

4 & 5. The surgery experience 6. Friends for life

7. Friends for life 8. Santa is coming to town
9. Jersey days

10 & 11. Jersey days
12 & 13. London memories

14. London memories 15. Lincoln lights
16 & 17. Toby Toblerone

18

18a

18b

The artwork I created
for Handmade by
Erika Daisy Wrate
18 Beatrice the
Butterfly
18a The Secret
Garden
18b Sid the Penguin
18c Beach huts

18c

The Annual Visit from Santa

When Sam and I were little, we were both a bit scared of Father Christmas. To fix this, Dad came up with a plan: he dressed up as Santa and visited us on Christmas Eve. Mum told us that Santa liked to check on all the children before Christmas morning, and every year we'd hear a knock on my bedroom door as proof.

Now, the idea of Dad dressing up as Santa sounds fairly simple, but in reality, he had a lot to do in a very short amount of time. After Sam and I had left out the carrots for the reindeer, the mince pie, and the glass of Baileys for Santa – yes, apparently, he can drink and drive – we were tucked into bed. Dad would say goodnight and pretend he was off to bed himself.

But instead of heading to sleep, he'd rush into the lounge, change into his Santa costume, shove a pillow up his jumper, take a bite out of the carrot, eat the mince pie, and down the Baileys (not that he had time to enjoy it). Then, he'd sprint around the garden just to reach the outside of my bedroom doors in time. And somehow, he managed to pull this off for years.

One particular year, he even came into my bedroom, held my hand, and asked if I'd been a good little girl. Of course, I said yes – but then I added, "You have really soft hands." I didn't even notice the pillow sticking out of his tummy!

As Sam got older, he eventually put two and two together and figured out what was really going on. But not me. I spent all of primary school telling everyone that Santa visited me and my brother every Christmas Eve.

Just before I started secondary school, Mum decided it was time I knew the truth. On my last day of primary, she took me home and gently explained that Santa wasn't real – that it had been Dad all along. My first reaction was to ask why they'd been lying to me.

But now, looking back, I'm so glad they did. It was such a magical surprise every year, and I love that Dad went to all that effort to make Christmas even more special for us.

Trips to Jersey

Ever since Sam and I were little – around three and five years old – Mum and Dad have taken us to visit my uncle George in Jersey. When I was small, we used to fly there, which was fairly easy. But as I got older and heavier, flying became more difficult, so we switched to taking the ferry.

The ferry ride was fun because it gave Sam and me the chance to explore (under supervision, of course – letting two kids wander off near the engine room would not have ended well). But it was also a bit stressful, as the whole trip – including the drive – took about ten hours.

While we were in Jersey, Mum and Dad would always take us to Jersey Zoo, and we'd visit George's café/restaurant, where we got loads of freebies! One year at the zoo, Sam and I couldn't stop laughing because we decided Dad looked a bit like the gorillas. It became a long-running family joke, and now, every time we see a gorilla – even just a statue – we can't help but compare it to Dad, much to his annoyance.

George's house is upside down, meaning the living space is on the top floor and the bedrooms are on the ground floor. At first, this wasn't really an issue, but as I got older, we had to start booking hotels to stay in, as I couldn't get upstairs anymore.

On one of our annual visits, we found out George's partner, Anna, was pregnant with a baby girl. It was such an exciting time for the family, and we couldn't wait to meet the newest addition!

When their baby, Florence, was a toddler, we went on a trip to the beach, all packed into George's van. Sam, Dad and Anna went for a swim in the sea, while Mum, George, Florence and I stayed in the van watching them from a distance.

The best part of the day for me, though, was when Anna left George in charge of feeding Flo her lunch – which, unfortunately for George, was spaghetti Bolognese. By the end of it, Florence's face was completely covered in tomato sauce, and she was giggling without a care in the world. George, on the other hand, looked less amused, clearly regretting his new role as lunchtime supervisor. It was hilarious to watch, and it's still one of my favourite memories from that trip!

Dad, the Sea and an Unexpected Surprise

During one of our trips to Jersey, something happened to Dad that we still laugh about to this day – well, all of us except Dad! It's one of those stories that gets funnier every time we tell it, although I'm pretty sure he might not agree.

On the boat journey, we were all on the lower level, enjoying the ride. Mum and I decided to leave Dad and Sam for a bit to browse the shops on board. We were gone for a little while, happily indulging in some retail therapy, completely unaware of the chaos unfolding in our absence.

When we came back to the boys, we were greeted by an unusual sight. Sam was sitting there, trying to stifle his laughter but failing miserably, while Dad sat in his chair looking utterly defeated. He had a box of tissues, three bags of sweets, and a brand-new shirt on.

Naturally, Mum and I started bombarding him with questions. What happened? Why are you wearing a new shirt? And why is

Sam laughing so hard? Through tears of laughter, Sam managed to choke out, "Someone just threw up on Dad."

At that point, I couldn't help but join in with the laughter. Poor Dad just sat there, wiping himself down with tissues, looking like he wanted to disappear.

Apparently, he had been leaning over the edge of the boat, peacefully enjoying the sea air. But, unbeknownst to him, a young boy on the level above was also leaning over the edge – but for a very different reason. According to Dad, the boy looked very green and was clearly seasick.

Before Dad even realised what was happening, he felt something falling on him. The young boy had thrown up.

The crew members, seeing what had happened, felt sorry for him and brought him a new shirt from the onboard shop so he could change. They also gave him a box of tissues and three bags of sweets as a sympathy gift, hoping to make up for the trauma!

Though Dad was horrified, the rest of us couldn't stop laughing, and honestly, we still can't. It's one of those family stories that always makes an appearance at gatherings, much to Dad's dismay.

Needless to say, Dad now double-checks what's above him before he leans over any railings!

London Visits and Family Time

In addition to our trips to Jersey, we also make regular visits to London to see my aunt, Abi, her husband, Flavio, and my cousins, Greta and Eva. We often venture into the heart of the city and enjoy the typical tourist attractions like the London Eye and Big Ben. It's always an exciting adventure, and even though navigating the crowds can be a challenge, it's fun to experience the sights with my family.

One year, we went to the *Wildlife Photographer of the Year* exhibition, which was a fantastic experience. It was amazing to see so many breathtaking images of animals and nature from around the world. Dad, being a photographer himself, couldn't resist joking that he could do better. At one point, he even asked us to take his photo in front of the sign that read Wildlife Photographer of the Year to pretend it was him!

I also have another aunt, Danielle, who lives in London and works as an editor. She's my dad's sister (Abi and George are on Mum's side) and often comes to visit us. During lockdown, she stayed with us for the entire period, which was lovely, as we got to spend so much time together.

Trips to Lincoln and Sleepovers at Sam's

When Sam turned 18, he started working for Dad at his factory in Newark. Since the daily commute was a bit of a trek, we decided he needed a place of his own in Lincoln to make things easier. We found a great spot for him in Burton Waters, a quiet area with canals and scenic views. It was the perfect choice, giving Sam a shorter commute and a lovely place to call home.

Whenever Mum and I head over for a sleepover at Sam's, we often make a day of it and visit Doddington Hall. It's one of our favourite places to go for breakfast, and we always enjoy browsing the little shops nearby. At Christmas, they even turn an entire shop into a Christmas wonderland – the Bauble Barn. It's like stepping into a holiday dream, full of festive decorations.

We also love walking around Lincoln, whether we're shopping or just taking in the sights. One of our traditions is visiting Lincoln Castle, especially during the Christmas Light Festival. The castle is lit up beautifully, and the light displays around the grounds are always so magical. Another regular stop is the cathedral. The views from there are stunning, and it's always peaceful.

In summer, we like to take a stroll to Sam's local pub for a drink and some food. The walk is so relaxing, with the canals and boats adding a serene vibe. When it's colder, we'll settle in for a cosy evening at Sam's with a takeaway and a good movie.

No matter the season, there's always something special about our trips to Lincoln. And of course, I look forward to my "hotel stay" at Sam's – it's always a treat!

Sundown Adventureland and the Yellow Brick Road

When Sam and I were younger, Grandad and Grandma used to take us to Sundown Adventureland, a little theme park that was perfect for kids. One of the things I remember most vividly was their version of the Yellow Brick Road from *The Wizard of Oz*. It was one of those iconic experiences where you could actually walk – or in my case, roll – down the road and meet characters like the Tin Man, the Scarecrow and the Lion.

The problem for me was, well, the people dressed in full-body costumes. As a kid, I was totally terrified of them (and honestly, a little bit now, too). So, instead of going down the road like everyone else, I'd take a little detour around the characters and enjoy the rest of the park. Grandad would always make sure we had an ice cream or snack, and we'd sit together watching other families brave the Yellow Brick Road, while I stayed firmly on the sidelines.

Eventually, after a few visits, Grandad and Grandma finally convinced me to give the road a try. Looking back, I have to admit it was pretty fun! But still, even now, if I saw a life-sized Tin Man walking towards me, I might hesitate just a little before stepping forward!

Family Holidays – Well Worth the Wait

Over the years, we've been on various holidays, mostly by car, but for one of them, my dad decided to take us barging in Berkshire. I don't think he fully realised how much work was involved. It turned out to be a lot of effort, but it was still a lovely holiday – just the four of us together.

We've also visited places like Bath, where we had the chance to explore the Roman Baths. It was a fascinating experience and definitely one of those trips that stands out in my memory.

Cornwall and Devon have also been holiday hotspots for us. The long car rides down aren't always the most fun, but they're well worth it for the breathtaking views and the memories we make.

Last year, we spent our summer holiday in Salcombe. We explored some great places while we were there, but I insisted we visit Paignton Zoo. Why? Because they have giraffes – and our local zoos and wildlife parks don't! Giraffes are one of my favourite animals, so missing the chance to see them just wasn't an option.

Meanwhile, my brother and dad decided to try paddle boarding and kayaking. They spent hours out on the water, attempting to balance on the paddle boards and steer the kayaks along the coastline. I was more than happy to watch from the shore, soaking up the sun and enjoying the view.

During a trip to Falmouth, we visited some beautiful gardens, including The Lost Gardens of Heligan, which were absolutely stunning. We also spent a day at the Eden Project, which was just as enjoyable – and not just because of the plants.

While walking past a large room at the Eden Project, we saw loads of kids building forts with sticks and fabric sheets. My dad instantly took a liking to the idea, grabbed Sam, and dove right in. He didn't just settle for a simple structure with three sticks and a sheet draped over the top – oh no. He went all out, collecting every spare stick and sheet in sight to build an enormous, intricate fort.

By the time he was halfway through, every child (and their parents) had stopped what they were doing to watch his creation take shape. At that point, it was less of a kids' activity and more of an engineering project!

Burghley House: Gardens, Mazes and Family Memories

We often go to a place in Stamford called Burghley House, which is always a nice spot to visit, especially for its beautiful gardens. One of the best bits is the mirror maze, which is always a laugh as you try to find your way through. We end up cracking up as we bump into our own reflections, thinking we've found the way out, only to realise we're still stuck. It's even funnier when we try to give each other directions – it always ends up making things more confusing!

Another fun part is the water features, where you have to try to get across without getting wet. Timing is everything! The fountains always seem to surprise you with sudden bursts of water, and it's a real test of patience and speed as you try to dash through without getting soaked. It's so satisfying when you make it through dry, and of course, someone always misjudges it and ends up with wet shoes, but that just makes it even funnier.

We usually visit in the summer, using Burghley House as a halfway point to meet my cousins who live in London. It's a great place to catch up, with loads of space to explore. The gardens are perfect for wandering around, and we always end up finding a quiet spot for a picnic, spreading out blankets and sharing homemade treats while we chat and relax in the sun.

Seals, Sand and Unforgettable Adventures

Mum has taken me on some truly unforgettable trips, but one place that sticks out in my memory is Donna Nook. She took me there to see the newborn baby seals – but I don't think anything could have prepared me for what we saw.

The whole area was absolutely swamped with seals – tiny, fluffy pups snuggling up to their mums, lazing on the sand and wobbling around like they were still figuring out how their flippers worked. It was like stepping into a real-life nature documentary, except instead of watching through a screen, we were right there, surrounded by what felt like thousands of seals living their best lives. The noises they made were a mix of adorable squeaks and loud, echoing calls – and we could have stood there watching them for hours without getting bored.

Some of the pups were so close to the viewing area that we could see every detail – from their whiskery faces to the soft, snowy fur they'd eventually shed as they grew older. Mum and I spent ages just watching them, pointing out the especially cute ones (which, to be honest, was all of them) and laughing whenever one of the pups did something silly, like rolling over too far and flopping onto its back.

Seeing them in the wild was magical – but we also often visit our local seal sanctuary, Natureland, where injured or abandoned seals are cared for. The team works so hard to nurse them back to health, feeding them, treating their wounds, and helping them build up their strength until they're ready to return to the sea. We've even been lucky enough to watch some of the releases – and seeing a seal shuffle down the beach, hesitate for a moment, and then disappear into the waves is incredibly moving. It's like watching the final chapter of their rescue story – knowing they're heading back to where they belong.

My Short-Lived Seal Career

When I was 17, I decided to try and get a job at Natureland, Skegness's famous seal sanctuary. I imagined myself as one of those people who walks around sharing facts and information about the seals. I've always loved animals, so I figured it would be my dream job. I pictured myself educating visitors, spending my days surrounded by nature, and doing something that really mattered. I was genuinely excited and thought it would be a great way to gain some experience while enjoying myself.

To my surprise, I actually got the job! However, things didn't quite go as planned. First of all, it turned out to be an unpaid position, which wasn't exactly what I was expecting. I had hoped for at least a little something to help cover my travel or maybe some pocket money, but I figured the experience alone would be worth it.

Then came the bigger issue: even though Orla – who was looking after me at the time – and I were both wearing the official Natureland uniform, no one seemed to notice us. Not a single person came up to ask about the seals. Instead, we just sat there in our designated spot, kind of in the background, waiting for something to happen. It felt a bit surreal to be right in the middle of the sanctuary, surrounded by these amazing animals, yet completely invisible to the crowds around us.

After a few sessions of sitting quietly, eating ice cream, and watching the visitors stroll past, I started to wonder if I was doing something wrong. Was it my approach? Were people just not in the mood to chat about seals? I kept hoping someone might come over and ask for a fun fact or show some curiosity – but no luck.

Eventually, I realised the job just wasn't what I had imagined. It wasn't the interactive, rewarding role I had pictured, and it didn't feel right to keep going if nothing was really happening. So, after some thought, I decided to hand in my badge and call it a day.

It may not have been the exciting seal-expert career I had dreamed of, but at least I gave it a try. And to be fair, I did get a few free ice creams out of it so it wasn't a total loss!

Discovering Musicals and the West End

As I got older, I became more and more interested in theatre shows – especially West End musicals. I've seen some amazing productions, including *Frozen* and *Matilda*, but one of my all-time favourites has to be *The Lion King*. The colours, the music, the acting – everything was incredible. But what really blew me away was the creativity behind the animal puppets.

Right at the start of the show, during the opening number 'Circle of Life', all the puppets came down the aisles, and seeing them up close was something else. They were huge – much bigger than I expected – and the detail was incredible. Giraffes towered over the audience, elephants walked past us, and for a moment, it really felt like we were in the African savanna. I just sat there completely awestruck.

After that, I was hooked. So now, as soon as I see something new coming to the West End that catches my eye, I tell Mum to get tickets straight away – no hesitation!

One time, Dad took us to see *The Play That Goes Wrong*. I was fairly young then, so most of the jokes went over my head, but even though I didn't fully get the humour, it was still a fun day out.

The shows are always amazing, but I love the trips themselves too. Since I'm usually driven everywhere, going on the train is a fun change. Sometimes, Danielle, Greta, Abi or other family members join us, which makes it even better.

Concerts and an Evolving Taste in Music

It's not just musicals – I've always had a deep love for music in general. My taste has always been a bit different from most people my age, mainly because of my dad's influence and his endless musical knowledge. I'm a big fan of artists like Amy Winehouse, Ray LaMontagne and Alicia Keys. I tend to go for what I call gentle music – blues, soul and jazz – the kind you can just sit with and get lost in.

When I was about 13, though, my music obsession took a different turn. I begged my parents to take me to see The Vamps, a boy band I absolutely adored at the time. Dad wasn't exactly thrilled at the idea, but after some serious persuasion, he gave in and took me. He went in grumbling about a night of screaming teenagers, but by the end of the concert, he'd bought nearly every piece of merchandise they had – including a winter hat that he still wears to this day!

Eventually, my music taste shifted again, and I started exploring other genres. I became a big fan of the TV show *Glee* and loved how they reworked familiar songs. Whenever I heard something I liked on the show, I'd track down the original version and add it to my playlist. That habit helped me discover a whole range of artists I probably wouldn't have found otherwise.

One of my favourite live music experiences happened more recently, when Dad took us to see Paloma Faith in Lincoln – a singer we all love. The concert itself was amazing, but the best part was that it meant we got to stay over at Sam's house – which is always a bonus in my book.

Whether it's a West End show, a live concert, or just a random song I've come across on TV, music has always been a huge part of my life. It's the soundtrack to my daydreams, my travels – and plenty of my family's funniest memories.

BBC Good Food Festival

A few years ago, Mum and Dad took me to the BBC Good Food Festival, where I got to watch – and even meet – two of my favourite cooks and bakers: Mary Berry and Jane Dunn from Jane's Patisserie. It was such an exciting experience, especially as they both gave live demonstrations where you could see them bake or cook something right in front of you. Watching them in action gave Mum and me loads of ideas and inspiration for things to try at home.

After their demos, there was a chance to buy their latest recipe books and get them signed – which, of course, I couldn't resist. I was completely starstruck, especially meeting Mary Berry, as I'd watched her on *The Great British Bake Off* for years. She was just as lovely and elegant in person as she is on TV. Jane Dunn was also really friendly, and it was brilliant to meet someone whose recipes I'd followed and enjoyed for so long.

Aside from the celebrity chefs, the festival itself was amazing. There were loads of incredible food stalls offering everything from homemade cakes and artisan bread to exotic street food from around the world. The smells alone were enough to make anyone hungry! We sampled a few different things and picked up some treats to take home. For lunch, we found a quiet spot to sit and enjoy some delicious food – the perfect break in the middle of such a busy, fun day.

That trip to the BBC Good Food Festival made me love baking and cooking even more. It was one of those days where I felt completely in my element – surrounded by amazing food and people who were just as passionate about it as I am.

Welcoming Toby, the Chocolate Labrador

When I was 11 and Sam was 14, we welcomed a puppy into the family. At the time, both of us were actually scared of dogs, so Mum and Dad decided that getting one might be the perfect way to show us there was nothing to be afraid of.

It also meant Mum and Dad couldn't come up with excuses to skip walks – whether it was a beach stroll or a trek through the fields near our house. In their eyes, it was a win-win.

We decided on a chocolate Labrador, and Dad came up with the perfect name – Toby. Or, as we liked to call him, Toblerone Toby.

Toby turned out to be a bit of a handful. We'd assumed Labradors would be easygoing and obedient, but Toby had other plans. He was full of energy and always up to something, usually involving chewing anything he could get his teeth on. Still, we didn't mind – it was all part of the chaos and joy of having a dog.

Grandma adored Toby, and the feeling was definitely mutual. He quickly figured out that all he had to do was look at her with his big eyes and she'd hand over a treat. No tricks, no commands – just a simple stare. She was his easiest target, and he made the most of it.

The number of dental sticks he got through in a single day was genuinely impressive – next-level levels of spoiling. That might explain why, in his later years, Toby carried a little extra weight. Dad would strongly disagree with this, of course, but let's be honest – Toby loved his snacks.

That said, there was one upside to Grandma's constant treating: every time Toby went to the vet, they commented on how brilliantly clean his teeth were. So yes, he might have been a bit rounder than average, but at least he had a dazzling smile.

Beyond his obsession with food, Toby was incredibly protective of me. He always seemed to know if I wasn't feeling well – it was like he had a sixth sense for it. The moment something felt off, he'd stay by my side until I was back to normal. Even then, he'd linger nearby, just keeping an eye on things. He wasn't just a pet – he was family. My four-legged guardian.

Toby needed lots of exercise, which meant plenty of walks – rain or shine. In summer, those walks were especially nice. I'd often meet everyone at the seafront café afterwards for a drink. We'd sit outside, sip milky coffees and, if it was lunchtime, share a plate of chips – with a sausage for Toby, of course.

We always joked that Toby was really the one in charge. If you asked him to do something he wasn't in the mood for, he'd shoot you a look that clearly said, "You must be joking." More often than not, it felt like he was the one walking us.

When Toby was 10, we had to say goodbye. He'd been such a constant part of our lives, and the house felt strange without him. For me especially, losing him was incredibly hard – he'd always been there, quietly watching over me and keeping me company. Letting him go wasn't easy, but we were grateful for the special years we shared with him.

Homemade Comfort: Meals with My Grandparents

When I was younger, we used to visit my Grandad and Grandma's house for Sunday lunch – and those visits were one of the highlights of my week. In my opinion, Grandma was one of the best cooks ever. Her meals were always amazing, and her desserts were something else entirely. I had three favourites and could never choose between them: apple pie, crumble, and slices of fruit with a caramel sauce.

But those lunches weren't just about the food. They were about spending time together, chatting around the table and enjoying each other's company. Toby often came along with us and would settle himself under the table as soon as we arrived. Even when food was being served, he'd usually doze off in complete comfort – though we were fairly sure it was all part of a clever plan to score leftovers. Sure enough, once the plates were cleared, Grandma would sneak him a few treats.

Looking back, I feel incredibly lucky to have those memories – and I genuinely don't believe any dessert will ever top Grandma's.

After she passed away, I decided to go through her collection of recipes – a well-loved file stuffed with pages cut from magazines and newspapers. I tried to recreate some of her dishes, but no matter how closely I followed the instructions, they never turned out quite the same. One of the recipes I saved was for a caramel nut dessert. A couple of years ago, I gave it a try – but I added too much salt and completely ruined it. I was so disappointed, but it reminded me just how effortlessly perfect her cooking always was.

Crafting Memories: Jewellery, Baking and Getting Creative

Over the years, Mum and I have done lots of art and craft workshops together in various places. We've always loved getting creative, whether it's painting, pottery, or even candle making. A couple of years ago, while scrolling through Facebook, Mum came across a post about the Lincoln School of Jewellery, which offers jewellery-making workshops. As soon as she showed it to me, we knew we had to book one.

The first workshop we chose was a ring-making class. We picked this one because I've always struggled to find rings small enough to fit my fingers, so the idea of making one myself was really exciting. The workshop was amazing – we got to do everything, from cutting the metal to hammering in a textured effect. We also learned how to shape and solder the ring together before polishing it to perfection. It was such a fun experience, and the best part was going home with a brand-new, shiny ring that fitted my finger perfectly. I loved having something handmade that was completely unique to me.

After that, we decided to return for another workshop – this time making a necklace. Just like with the rings, we got to design our own pendants from scratch, shaping and texturing the metal to create something equally unique. It was so much fun to experiment with different techniques and watch the necklace come to life. Every time I wear it now, I'm reminded of the experience.

Our creative workshops haven't been limited to jewellery making. We've also attended several cookery classes in Lincoln. So far, we've taken courses in patisserie and chocolate making. In the patisserie class, we learned how to make beautiful pastries and delicate desserts, while the chocolate-making class involved creating our own truffles – definitely a highlight.

Doing these workshops together has become a bit of a tradition for us, and we're always on the lookout for new ones to try. Not only is it a great way to learn new skills, but it's also a lovely way to spend quality time together, making memories (and, in some cases, delicious treats) along the way.

My Creative Journey: Handmade By EDW

I've always been a creative person – from scrapbooking and bullet journaling to drawing and painting. After I left school, I began painting more regularly, especially using watercolours. As I built up a collection of pieces, friends and family started encouraging me to sell my artwork as cards and prints. Sam even suggested I could set up a subscription service, where people would receive a set number of cards or prints each month. So, I decided to go for it and launched my own small business: *Handmade by Erika Daisy Wrate* – or *Handmade by EDW.*

As part of the subscription, I chose to donate a portion of the proceeds to Muscular Dystrophy UK – a cause that's close to my heart. I do all my artwork in my home office, where I've got a shelf (put up by Dad!) to display some of my favourite pieces. A few of my paintings are even framed and hanging in my bedroom.

When I first started the business, I wasn't sure how I'd manage everything alongside my other commitments, including my sessions with my home tutor. But over time, I've grown more confident and found a rhythm that works. A lot of my inspiration comes from places I've visited – especially for my landscape paintings. One of my favourite techniques is wet-on-wet, which creates soft blends and smooth transitions across the page.

I've had some lovely messages from customers – in person, over social media, and by email – saying how much they enjoy receiving my artwork. Knowing that something I've created can brighten someone's day is one of the best feelings, and it motivates me to keep going.

Looking ahead, I'd love to expand the business further. One of my future goals is to take part in craft markets and events, where I can meet customers face-to-face and connect with other creatives. I think it would be such a nice way to grow Handmade by EDW and share my work with even more people.

Turning Dreams into Reality

For my 18th birthday, Mum gave me a bangle engraved with the quote: *"Dreaming is a form of planning."* Those words really stuck with me. Mum and I have always been big dreamers – whether it's a trip to the West End or something more ambitious, we spend a lot of time talking about what we'd love to do and figuring out how to make it happen.

That quote sums up exactly how we go about things. For us, dreaming isn't just wishful thinking – it's the starting point. It's not about sitting back and hoping things work out, but about putting a plan in place and finding a way to make it real.

Special Birthday Memories

Thanks to my family – especially Mum and Dad – my birthdays have always been fantastic. But there are certain birthdays that really stick out in my memory.

For my fifth birthday, my grandma booked tickets to see *Disney on Ice* in Nottingham and arranged for us to travel there in a limousine. It was such a lovely surprise, and the whole experience felt incredibly fancy! I remember sitting in the limo, surrounded by twinkling lights and soft leather seats, feeling like a celebrity. The excitement built as we got closer to the theatre – I couldn't wait to see all my favourite Disney characters perform on the ice.

However, when we arrived, things didn't quite go to plan. While everyone else eagerly took their seats, Mum and I stayed behind in the corridor. As much as I loved Disney, there was just one small problem – I was still terrified of people dressed in full costumes. Suddenly, the thought of seeing giant versions of Mickey, Minnie and the princesses overwhelmed me, and my excitement turned into sheer panic.

No matter how hard Mum tried to convince me to go in, I just couldn't do it. She reassured me again and again, telling me how magical the show was and how much fun everyone was having inside – but I was still too nervous. So instead of watching the performance with my family, I spent most of the time sitting in the hallway, trying to muster the courage to go in.

Every now and then, I'd peek through the door, catch a glimpse of the dazzling lights and hear the music and cheers from the crowd. I wanted so badly to join in the excitement, but my fear held me back. Mum was incredibly patient, never once making me feel bad for missing the show. She sat with me and talked me through it, and even though I didn't get to see much of *Disney on Ice*, I still remember that day as special – not because of the show, but because of the effort my grandma went to and the way Mum stayed by my side the whole time.

For my 10th birthday, my dad organised a birthday party photoshoot for me and all my friends. He set up loads of balloons in the studio, including a gigantic number ten, and I felt like a superstar! We had an absolute blast, and it's one of those birthdays I'll never forget. He even made a red carpet for us to walk down.

Another birthday that stands out was more recent – my 21st. This one was especially memorable because we had loads of people there, including my cousins, aunts, uncles, friends, my brother and even some of my carers.

One of the highlights of the party was when Dad made these giant skis that could fit about four pairs of feet. We turned it into a race, and all you could hear was people shouting, "Left up!" and "Right up!" – it was so much fun.

After we'd finished racing in the garden and had eaten at a long trestle table set up outside, we all headed to the pub – or as we like to call it, Fen Lodge. We cranked up the music, and that's when the party really began. As a surprise, my brother and Dad had gone above and beyond and secretly decorated the pub in advance. They even covered part of the ceiling in balloons! It was a total surprise when we walked in, and the atmosphere was incredible. The whole day was filled with laughter and love – the perfect way to celebrate with the people I'm closest to.

Lockdown Fun

During the first coronavirus lockdown in 2020, like everyone else, we were confined to our home and quickly ran out of things to do. So, I came up with the idea of Monopoly Mondays. Each week, we'd head into the cinema room and play Monopoly on my Nintendo Switch, projecting it onto the big screen. But, of course, Dad being Dad, insisted it wasn't a proper game unless we put money on it. I think he regretted that suggestion almost immediately – because I ended up winning quite a few games!

We also started having movie nights at the weekends, and to avoid any arguments about what to watch, we came up with Film Club. The rules were simple: whoever picked the film didn't get to vote, and the rest of us rated it out of ten. If the film scored an average of seven or more, the picker got to choose the next week's movie. If not, it was someone else's turn. Surprisingly, this system actually worked really well!

As lockdown went on, these little traditions became something to look forward to. They gave us structure, lightened the mood and brought a lot of laughter – whether through the chaos of Monopoly or debating movie scores. Those quirky routines helped keep things fun and gave us something to bond over when the world outside felt so uncertain.

One day, Sam and I were left to entertain ourselves while Mum and Dad were busy doing jobs in the garden. Sam came up with a new activity he promised would be fun – and only "a little bit messy". He introduced me to something called pendulum painting. Although I was intrigued, I double-checked: "Are you sure this isn't going to be a mess?" He reassured me it would be fine.

We set everything up in my bedroom – grabbing a long piece of thick string, four empty plastic bottles, and several pots of washable paint. We taped the bottles together, poked holes in the bottoms, tied the string to them, and suspended it from the ceiling track. Then we placed four blank canvases on the floor, surrounded by sheets of newspaper, and started swinging the paint-filled bottles in all directions – forward, backward, left, right, and everywhere in between.

Unsurprisingly, Sam had completely lied about the mess! There was paint everywhere. Luckily, the floor was tiled – if it had been carpeted, Mum and Dad definitely wouldn't have seen the funny side. When Mum eventually came in and saw the chaos, she declared that pendulum painting was definitely not a house-approved activity. "Maybe in the sheds next time," she said. Despite the mess, it was one of the most fun and creative things we did during lockdown.

Another highlight was discovering with Danielle a baking subscription box. Every month, we received a package containing a surprise recipe and all the pre-weighed dry ingredients, each neatly labelled in order. A few days before the box arrived, we'd get an email listing the extra (usually wet) ingredients we'd need, but the actual recipe remained a mystery until it arrived – adding to the excitement.

Each recipe was fun and delicious. Some favourites included a coffee and chocolate roulade and blueberry and white chocolate cupcakes. We looked forward to each month's delivery, and it quickly became one of our favourite things to do together.

Another Member Joins the Family

After a couple of years without a dog, I started to feel that the house needed a new addition. And although they didn't want to admit it, Mum and Dad needed a dog too – to get them back into walking and out of the house more. So, after a few weeks of gentle persuasion from me, we decided it was time to welcome another four-legged friend.

This time, we chose a Fox Red Labrador – a breed I didn't even know existed until we started researching. Once we'd found a litter, the fun part began: choosing a puppy. That was the easy bit. The harder part was agreeing on a name. We went through a long list, including Benny, Jasper and even Trevor (which was Dad's suggestion!). Eventually, we all agreed on the name Lenny.

While we waited to collect him, we made sure we had all the essentials ready – like a bed, some bowls, and of course, plenty of toys. And then, it was finally time to bring our new family member home.

I think we'd all forgotten just how much chaos – and hair – comes with having a dog, especially one that moults! But none of us regretted the decision for a second. This time around, we've been a bit more relaxed with the rules. Toby was never really allowed on the sofa, my bed, or upstairs. But with Lenny, a couple of those rules have quietly expired. He's now allowed on the sofas, and –under supervision – he's even allowed on my bed for cuddles. That said, the upstairs ban still stands (for now!).

Lenny is very much a sea dog, especially if there are tennis balls involved. And when he gets a bit restless at home, Mum takes a bunch of dog balls and a tennis racket into the garden and launches them as far as she can. Lenny races off after them with boundless enthusiasm – although he rarely brings them back. Instead, he just sits, tail wagging, ready for the next one.

He's a total delight and the perfect addition to our family.

19 & 20. The big birthday
21, 22, 23 & 24. Family holidays

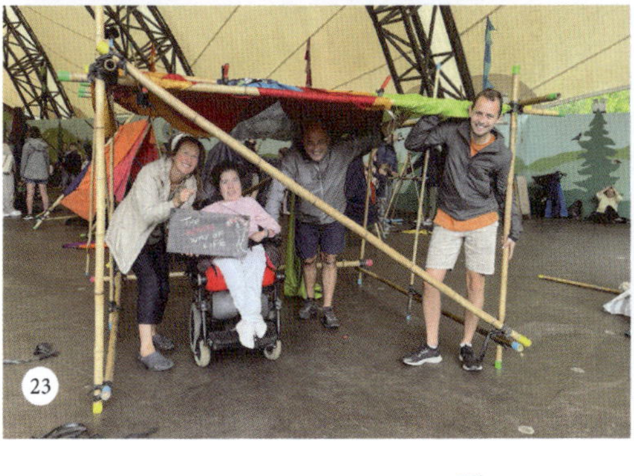

25 & 26. Lenny
27. Keeping traditions alive

28 & 29. *Keeping traditions alive*

30. Humpty 31 & 32. Fun times with Eva

33. Fun times with Eva 34. The Skegness SO Festival

35. Another New Year fancy dress party 36. Parrot zoo surprise
37. Center Parcs merriments 38. Barney 39. The cosy Cotswolds

Keeping Traditions Alive

Over the years, we've had so many fun family traditions, especially around Christmas and New Year. Most of them were started by my grandma, and after she passed away, we made sure to keep them alive – and even created a few new ones of our own!

One of Grandma's most impressive traditions was the Boxing Day buffet. Every year, we'd have family friends over, including my dad's best friend from school, and Grandma would lay out a huge spread. There were freshly made salads, bowls of crisps, a cheese board, homemade cakes, and even an alcohol-soaked Christmas cake. It was like a second Christmas feast! As I got older, I started to suspect that Grandma chose a buffet so she could enjoy the party (and a few glasses of fizz) without stressing about cooking.

After she died, I suggested we carry on the buffet tradition to keep that special part of Grandma with us. We all agreed, though these days we do it on a smaller scale. We quickly realised we were only getting through half the food, and Mum would spend the week trying to finish off the leftovers!

Another tradition we've kept alive involves pyjamas. Every Christmas Eve, Grandma would give us all a new pair of festive pyjamas to wear that night and into Christmas morning. I really wanted to continue the tradition, but as a student, I couldn't afford to buy six pairs of pyjamas every year. So, I came up with the idea of a Secret Santa pyjama exchange. That way, we all still get new pyjamas, but each of us only has to buy one pair. We even pick a theme each year to make it more fun – though some of us don't always stick to it! One year, my grandad decided to buy his person an animal onesie, which hasn't been seen since!

One of my favourite recent traditions is our New Year's Eve Murder Mystery Party. All the family comes over – my cousins, aunts and uncles – and we dress up as assigned characters. Some people take their costumes very seriously, which makes it even more hilarious. We even match the food to the theme of the mystery! So far, we've done *Murder on the Titanic, Murder on the Train,* and a Dickens-themed *Christmas Murder.*

One of the best parts of the night is when Dad takes a group photo of all of us in costume and adds a themed background to match the mystery. It's a fun way to capture the night and see how ridiculous (or impressive) our outfits are.

After the murder mystery, we head into the cinema room to watch a slideshow I put together with photos from the past year. My cousins even send me their pictures to include. It's such a lovely way to look back at everything we've done – all the memories we've made and the places we've been.

After the slideshow, we finish the night with a quiz. It usually has rounds like *Guess the Movie from the Photo* or *Finish the Song,* and we all get far too competitive. Although quite a few people (mentioning no names!) sneak off to bed before the countdown to the new year. They miss the final moments, but it's all part of the fun. Those of us who stay up make the most of it, laughing and enjoying the last bit of the year before ringing in the new one.

Christmas Eve is another special tradition. Every year, we meet up with Gill, Neil, Emily and Alice for an evening of festive fun. We exchange gifts, enjoy a lovely dinner together, and spend the night chatting and laughing. It's such a nice way to kick off Christmas, and we always make sure to snap a few photos to remember the night.

A couple of weeks before Christmas, me, Mum, Dad, Sam, Danielle and Grandad get together for a Christmas card competition. We all design and make our own cards, and Neil (being an architect with a good eye for design) is the official judge. It started as a fun little idea, but now it's become a full-on competition – and we all take it very seriously.

These traditions, old and new, are such a huge part of what makes the holidays special for us. Whether it's a Boxing Day buffet, a new pair of pyjamas, or solving a murder mystery in full costume, each one is a little reminder of the love, laughter and chaos that makes our family so unique. They bring us together, year after year, and I wouldn't have it any other way.

Humpty: The Unexpected Mascot

In 2020, just before the first lockdown, my dad and his business partner, Glyn, were on the hunt for a mascot for their company. After a few weeks of searching, they came across an auction selling the original Humpty Dumpty teddy from the children's TV show *Play School*. Intrigued by the nostalgia and uniqueness, they attended the auction – and ended up winning Humpty. Just like that, the business had a new mascot.

The plan was to take Humpty into local primary schools as a fun, friendly face to promote the company. But there was one major flaw – none of the children had a clue who he was. Even my brother and I weren't entirely sure. It turned out that while Humpty and *Play School* were iconic for a certain generation – kids of the '60s, '70s and '80s – the show had long vanished from TV.

Humpty was instantly recognisable to the parents and teachers, who lit up with excitement and shared fond memories. But to the kids, he was just a random, egg-shaped teddy with no obvious significance.

The contrast was hilarious. The adults were thrilled to have a cuddle with Humpty, while the children just stared in confusion, wondering what all the fuss was about. Despite the generational gap, Humpty became a quirky and entertaining part of Dad's business story – even if he turned out to be more of a hit with the grown-ups than the kids!

Fun Times with Eva

Several times a year, one of my cousins, Eva, comes to stay and helps my mum look after me. We always end up doing really fun things together while she's here, like having picnics in the park. A couple of summers ago, we made sandwiches for one of those picnics, wrapped them in tinfoil, and used alphabet sticks to add our names to them. We often go strawberry picking too – and maybe pinch a few as we go around (shhh, don't tell anyone!).

We also enjoy visiting our local wildlife parks and a seal sanctuary near our house. Another favourite spot to take Eva is The Kinema In The Woods – a beautiful cinema about an hour away, surrounded by trees and lovely little walkways. They even have an organ player who rises from the floor during the intermission! My mum and I often go there together, too, and it's always a lovely experience.

Sometimes when Eva's here, we take her to the SO Festival – a fantastic event filled with acrobatic performances and street acts, much like a carnival. In 2012, when the festival was first held, my dad's photography company was hired to take a special photograph of the event using a camera mounted on an extended pole. Interestingly, the Olympic torch was also being carried through the town on the same day – adding another special touch to the occasion.

Adventures at The Parrot Zoo

We often visit Lincolnshire Wildlife Park – also known as The Parrot Zoo – which has changed and grown over the years to accommodate a variety of animals, including rescued Bengal tigers. I remember one visit when a tiger was lounging right on the windowsill – seeing one up close was both awe-inspiring and a little intimidating! While Mum and I kept our distance, we noticed a little girl, no older than five, pressed right up against the glass, her hands on the window. You could see her mother growing anxious, and before long, she gently led her daughter away to see another animal. As they walked off, we overheard the girl say, "I like it," which made Mum and me quietly chuckle. We couldn't help but whisper to each other that she might feel differently if the tiger ever got out!

The park always seems to have something memorable going on. One year, a parrot had to be put in isolation for swearing at customers – and on the flip side, another parrot became a bit of a star after going viral for singing Beyoncé's hit 'If I Were a Boy'. It's kind of amazing to see how much personality these birds have – you never quite know what to expect when visiting!

Now, if we ever manage to persuade the boys to come with us, I often catch Dad and Sam quietly swearing back at the parrots – almost like they're trying to get even. It's become a bit of a running joke, and honestly, it's hard not to laugh when you hear them muttering under their breath as the parrots squawk away!

Every visit leaves us with a new story to tell – whether it's tigers in windows, singing parrots, or our own family antics. It's one of those places that never gets old, and I'm sure we'll keep going back for years to come.

Center Parcs Trips and Traditions

For the past few years, we've taken many trips to Center Parcs – usually in December, around Christmas time. It's always magical because they decorate the whole place with beautiful Christmas lights, and even as you drive in, you're surrounded by trees covered in twinkling lights.

On our first festive trip there, we were given the option to have a Christmas tree set up for us. But no – Dad wanted to do it 'Wrate style'. Instead of a traditional tree, he brought along a blow-up one. At first, everyone except Dad was unsure about it, but it quickly became part of our tradition. Another tradition that's formed is Eva joining us – which makes the trips even more special.

One of the most memorable moments from that first Center Parcs trip happened at the swimming pool, and it's certainly not something Dad or I will ever forget! Because of my disability, I always need to be held by someone when I'm in the water. During this particular swim, Mum left Dad holding me while she, Eva and Sam went off to try some of the water slides.

What none of us had realised was that this particular pool had a wave machine – which they activated with a loud Tarzan sound effect. One minute, Dad and I were calmly floating in the centre of the pool – and the next, the waves came. And they kept coming.

Dad used one arm to hold me as tightly as possible and the other to shuffle us towards the shallow area where we'd be safe. It wasn't exactly a relaxing swim! To make matters worse, as Dad was shuffling through the water, his trunks started slipping down. By the time we reached the shallow end, he was just hoping the lifeguard wasn't paying too much attention to that area!

When Mum, Eva and Sam returned, Dad and I were completely dishevelled and out of breath. Needless to say, I haven't been back in that swimming pool since. I've stuck to the spa pool – where there are no unexpected waves and definitely no wardrobe malfunctions!

One of the highlights of these trips is the festive firework evening. Towards the end of the show, Santa appears on a jet ski riding across the lake. We can't help but giggle at how odd and unexpected it looks – but it's become something we look forward to every year.

When I turned 21 in July 2023, we decided to switch things up and visit Center Parcs in the summer instead. It was a fun experience – especially since, most mornings, we had ducks waddling straight into our lodge. But as we drove home, we all agreed that while it had been great, we still preferred it in the winter.

A Cosy Cotswolds Getaway

In November 2024, me, Mum, Dad, Sam, Lenny and all of our extended family went on a trip to the Cotswolds, where we stayed in a beautiful rented house. It was the perfect getaway – both peaceful and scenic – and a great way for all of us to catch up and spend quality time together. The house itself was lovely, with plenty of space for everyone to relax and enjoy themselves. They even had an Aga, which made the whole place feel warm and cosy – especially on those chilly November evenings.

We spent our days exploring the charming villages, taking in the stunning countryside views, and – of course – indulging in some great food. We visited some lovely local pubs and restaurants, and also cooked up some fantastic meals ourselves, making the most of the huge kitchen and enjoying family dinners together.

Some members of the family even went out for local runs, taking advantage of the beautiful countryside routes. Back at the house, we discovered a treasure trove of board games, including classics like Jenga, which brought plenty of laughs and competitive moments. There was also a table tennis table that everyone enjoyed – with matches getting quite intense as we battled it out for the win.

One of the highlights was when we found some plastic cups and a hockey stick. We used the cups to create a makeshift obstacle course, using the hockey stick to move a ball around them. It sounds simple, but it was so much fun! Later on, we also played a game called *Cups*. To explain how it works – if there are, say, thirteen people playing, you set up eleven cups in a line on the table. Six people stand on either side of the table, and one person stands at the foot of it, acting as the caller. The caller shouts things like "ears", "nose", "head", "toes" – and everyone has to touch that body part. But as soon as they say "cups", it's a race to grab one as quickly as possible. Whoever misses out is eliminated. This continues until only two people and one cup remain – then it's war! Whoever grabs the last cup wins.

After playing, we couldn't stop laughing at how many people accidentally scratched each other amidst the chaos!

Evenings were filled with games, movie nights, and plenty of reminiscing about old memories – while making new ones. It was one of those holidays where everything just felt easy and enjoyable, and I'll always look back on it as a special time with my family.

Living Room Concerts and Off-Key Duets

When I was younger, like most kids, I asked for a Nintendo Wii – and I was lucky enough to get one. One of my absolute favourite games to play was the *X Factor* game, where you could pretend you were actually competing on the TV show. You got to do everything from the nerve-wracking auditions to the dramatic boot camp, all the way to the grand finale. The game even had avatars that looked like the real-life judges. We had the whole setup at my grandparents' house, complete with a microphone and microphone stand, so I could go all out with my performances. My go-to song was Queen's 'Radio Ga Ga', but we also sang songs like 'Ruby' by the Kaiser Chiefs and 'Hey Jude' by the Beatles. We'd turn the living room into our own personal arena, and every performance felt like a headline show.

I often played the game with Danielle, who also loved getting involved, even though her singing was sometimes a bit tuneless (she would completely disagree, of course), and we'd end up laughing so much that we could barely get through a song. We'd argue over who was the real star of the show, and even though the game would score our performances, we were both convinced the system was rigged if we didn't win.

Sometimes, Grandma and Grandad would pop their heads into the room to watch, clapping for us at the end of each song as if we'd just delivered a Grammy-worthy performance. Those living room concerts could go on for hours, and we'd only stop when our voices were completely gone (or when the adults finally begged for peace and quiet).

It was such a fun way to spend time together, and even now, thinking back to those mini living room concerts brings back some of the best memories. It didn't matter that we weren't the most gifted singers in the world – it was all about the fun, laughter, and pretending we were popstars for a little while.

Barney the Dinosaur

I was at home working with my carer one day when I heard Mum's exasperated voice asking, "What on earth have you brought home this time, Martin?"

It turns out that while out with Sam, Dad spotted a massive statue of Barney the Dinosaur in a charity shop window and, of course, he couldn't resist bringing it back with him. It was huge, clunky and slightly terrifying, but Dad thought it was hilarious. That's when he and Sam came up with a wild idea to turn Barney into a Christmas tradition to rival Santa!

Every year on Christmas Eve, under the cover of darkness, Dad and Sam would dress Barney up as something ridiculous, sneak over to our neighbours' house – where Neil, Gill, Alice and Emily live – and leave him in their garden.

Then the neighbours decided to play along. They'd keep Barney for a while, dress him up as something equally comical, and then secretly return him to our garden. Sometimes they would hold onto him for a whole year, but other times he'd make a surprise appearance at Easter – complete with bunny ears and a basket of plastic eggs. Mum used to joke that Gill probably didn't want Barney in her garden any more than she did, so she'd pass him back as soon as she could.

Over the years, Barney was transformed into everything from a prehistoric snooker player to a poorly spray-painted Grinch.

But as time wore on, his once-vibrant purple hue faded, and he started to look more like a relic from a forgotten theme park than a beloved children's character. Eventually, he was retired to one of the sheds, where he now rests in peace (or pieces). Mum had absolutely no remorse as she announced, "RIP, Barney!"

ABBA-solutely Living My Best Life

Over the past few years, I've been lucky enough to go on some amazing holidays and trips – from family getaways to Bath, Jersey and Cornwall, to city breaks in London with Mum for sightseeing, visiting my cousins, or catching a show at the theatre. One of our most recent and memorable London trips was when Mum, Danielle and I went to see *Mamma Mia* in the West End.

The whole experience was fantastic, right from the moment we arrived in the capital. Mum had booked us into a very fancy hotel called the Waldorf, where we were greeted with a glass of Prosecco on arrival. We always try to book a hotel close to the theatre to avoid lots of walking or public transport, but this time we outdid ourselves – the theatre was literally the next door along! We couldn't believe how close we were; it was the most convenient setup ever.

The show was a matinee, so we had plenty of time to enjoy the performance and still have a relaxing evening afterwards. Every musical I've seen so far has been amazing, but *Mamma Mia* was extra special because it featured all my favourite ABBA songs, along with stunning choreography, acting and singing. The funniest part of the day happened before the show even started. Mum spotted a poster outside the theatre showing a scene from "Lay All Your Love on Me," with lots of male dancers in tight swimsuits. She turned to me with a big smile and said,

"No wonder you wanted to see this show, Erika!" We all had a good laugh about that, and when the show announcer warned the audience that there would be plenty of dancers in swimming trunks, none of us were complaining!

After the show, we recharged in our lovely hotel room before heading down to the restaurant to meet Greta and Abi for dinner. The following morning, we woke up to one of the best breakfasts we've ever had – a huge, beautifully set buffet.

Later that morning, Mum and Danielle took me to St Pancras station to see where you catch the Eurostar to Paris. Mum knows how much I want to visit the French capital, so she wanted to show me exactly how we'd get there when the time comes. When we arrived, I mentioned that it seemed oddly quiet for such a famous station. That's when Mum and Danielle explained that all the trains to Paris had been cancelled because they'd found an unexploded Second World War bomb near the tracks over on the other side of the water. It was surreal to think something like that could still trigger transport chaos after all these years, but it definitely made for an interesting story to tell!

After our little detour, we went to the Royal Opera House, where Danielle took us to the top floor to have a drink and enjoy the gorgeous view over Covent Garden. Mum and I both agreed we'd love to come back to see a performance – maybe something like *The Nutcracker* at Christmas. It felt like such a special place, and we were already planning our next trip before we'd even set off for home.

When it was time to head back to Skegness, we made our way to King's Cross Station, where the access team informed us that the only available wheelchair space on our train was in first class! So, we ended up travelling in luxury, with complimentary drinks and freshly made sandwiches. It was the perfect end to an already amazing trip.

While looking through the photos from our adventure, I couldn't help but start thinking ahead. A week later, after reliving all the highlights, I remembered Danielle showing me the trailer for *Back to the Future: The Musical*. I mentioned it to Mum, and without skipping a beat, she said, "Let's book it!" And just like that, another adventure was in the works.

Who knows what's next? But one thing's for sure: we'll be booking tickets, packing bags and creating memories – one show at a time.

Epilogue

Looking back over everything that's happened so far – from zooming around in my first electric wheelchair and accidentally becoming the world's worst toe-slayer, to dreaming up wild plans with Mum that once felt impossible – it's fair to say it's been one heck of a ride. Sure, there were a few bumps along the way (literally and figuratively), but I wouldn't change a thing.

I've learned a lot – like how to turn dreams into reality and how to avoid knocking into too many door frames. Starting my own business has been a huge challenge, but it's also reminded me that if you dream big enough and work hard enough, things have a habit of falling into place.

Who knows what's next? All I know is that I'll keep dreaming and planning – probably running over a few toes along the way. I'm ready for whatever comes, and I'll face it with a smile, plenty of determination, and maybe a few more accidental furniture collisions. And hey, if nothing else, at least it'll be entertaining!

So, here's to the next chapter – may it bring fewer broken cupboards, more London adventures, and maybe a little less destruction around the house. Whatever happens, I'm excited for it.

Acknowledgements

I'm incredibly grateful to my family for their endless support and encouragement, and for all the experiences that have shaped my writing. Your belief in me has been my foundation, and you've inspired me every step of the way.

A heartfelt thank you to my Auntie Danielle, whose help in editing and publishing this book made my dream of becoming an author a reality. Your patience and dedication have meant the world to me.

Lastly, I must thank the technology that has allowed me to write this autobiography independently. The tools I used helped to bring my thoughts to life, making it possible for me to tell my story in my own way, on my own terms.

Printed in Dunstable, United Kingdom